One Hundred and One
Best Rhymes
for Children

One Hundred and One Best Rhymes for Children

Selected by
Holly Pell McConnaughy

BARNES
&NOBLE
BOOKS
NEW YORK

Contents

One Hundred and One
Best Rhymes
for Children

I'm Glad

I'm glad the sky is painted blue,
And earth is painted green,
With such a lot of nice fresh air
All sandwiched in between.

Hickory, Dickory

Hickory, dickory, dock,
The mouse ran up the clock;
    The clock struck one,
    The mouse ran down,
Hickory, dickory, dock.

Higgledy Piggledy

Higgledy piggledy,
    Here we lie,
Picked and plucked,
    And put in a pie!

Rub-A-Dub-Dub

Rub-a-dub-dub,
Three men in a tub,
    And who do you think they be?
The butcher, the baker,
The candlestick maker;
    Turn 'em out, knaves all three!

Mary

Mary, Mary, quite contrary,
    How does your garden grow?
With cockle-shells and silver bells
    And columbines all in a row.

Bobby Shaftoe

Bobby Shaftoe's gone to sea,
Silver buckles at his knee;
When he comes back, he'll marry me,
  Bonny Bobby Shaftoe.

Bobby Shaftoe's fat and fair,
Combing down his yellow hair;
He's my love for evermair,
  Bonny Bobby Shaftoe.

Peter, Pumpkin Eater

Peter, Peter, pumpkin eater,
  Had a wife and couldn't keep her;
He put her in a pumpkin shell
  And there he kept her very well.

Little Miss Muffit

Little Miss Muffit,
Sat on a tuffit,
   Eating of curds and whey;
There came a great spider
That sat down beside her,
   And frightened Miss Muffit away.

Jack Spratt

Jack Spratt could eat no fat,
    His wife could eat no lean;
And so betwixt them both, you see,
    They lick'd the platter clean.

Tom the Piper's Son

Tom he was the piper's son,
 He learn'd to play when he was young,
But the only tune that he could play
 Was, "Over the hills and far away."

Peter White

Peter White will ne'er go right;
 Would you know the reason why?
He follows his nose where'er he goes,
 And that stands all awry.

For Want of a Nail

For want of a nail, the shoe was lost;
For want of the shoe, the horse was lost;
For want of the horse, the rider was lost;
For want of the rider, the battle was lost;
For want of the battle, the kingdom was lost;
And all for the want of a horseshoe nail.

Sing, Sing

Sing, sing, what shall I sing?
     The cat has eaten the pudding-string!
Do, do, what shall I do?
     The cat has bitten it quite in two.

Dickery Dare

Dickery, dickery, dare,
　　The pig flew up in the air;
The man in brown soon brought him down,
　　Dickery, dickery, dare.

Pussy-Cat, Pussy-Cat

Pussy-cat, pussy-cat, where have you been?
    I've been to London to look at the queen.
Pussy-cat, pussy-cat, what did you there?
    I frighten'd a little mouse under the chair.

Little Wee Dog

Oh where and oh where is my little wee dog?
  Oh where and oh where is he?
With his ears cut short and his tail cut long,
  Oh where and oh where can he be?

Jack a Nory

I'll tell you a story
    About Jack a Nory, —
And now my story's begun:
    I'll tell you another
About Jack and his brother, —
    And now my story's done.

Solomon Grundy

Solomon Grundy,
Born on a Monday,
Christened on Tuesday,
Married on Wednesday,
Took ill on Thursday,
Worse on Friday,
Died on Saturday,
Buried on Sunday.
This is the end of
Solomon Grundy.

Little Jack Horner

Little Jack Horner sat in the corner
    eating a Christmas pie;
He put in his thumb,
    and he took out a plum,
And said, "What a good boy am I!"

Wishes

If wishes were horses,
  Beggars would ride;
If turnips were watches,
  I'd wear one by my side.

The Merchants of London

Hey diddle, dinkety, poppety, pet,
    The merchants of London they wear scarlet,
Silk in the collar, and gold in the hem,
    So merrily march the merchant men.

A Dillar, a Dollar

A dillar, a dollar,
    A ten o'clock scholar,
What makes you come so soon?
    You used to come at ten o'clock
But now you come at noon.

Fool

Fool, fool, come out of school,
And point me out the Golden Rule!

Brow Brinky

Brow brinky,
Eye winky,
Chin choppy,
Nose noppy,
Cheek cherry,
Mouth merry.

Mix a Pancake

Mix a pancake,
Stir a pancake,
    Pop it in the pan.
Fry a pancake,
Toss a pancake,
    Catch it if you can.

Mr. East

Mr. East gave a feast;
Mr. North laid the cloth;
Mr. West did his best;
Mr. South burnt his mouth
With eating a cold potato.

Cross Patch

Cross patch,
Draw the latch,
   Sit by the fire and spin;
Take a cup,
And drink it up,
   And call your neighbours in.

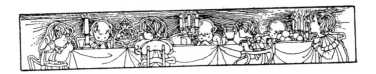

As I Went to Bonner

As I went to Bonner,
  I met a pig without a wig,
Upon my word of honour.

My Black Hen

Higglepy, Piggleby,
 My black hen,
She lays eggs
 For gentlemen;
Sometimes nine,
 And sometimes ten,
Higglepy, Piggleby,
 My black hen.

To Market

To market, to market, to buy a fat pig.
  Home again, home again, dancing a jig;
To market, to market, to buy a fat hog,
  Home again, home again, jiggety-jog.

The Old Man

There was an old man,
And he had a calf,
   And that's half;
He took him out of the stall,
And tied him to a wall,
   And that's all.

Shall We Go Shearing

"Old woman, old woman,
　　shall we go shearing?"
"Speak a little louder, sir,
　　I am very thick of hearing."
"Old woman, old woman,
　　shall I love you dearly?"
"Thank you, kind sir,
　　I hear you very clearly."

Tweedle-Dum
and Tweedle-Dee

Tweedle-dum and Tweedle-dee
    Resolved to have a battle,
For Tweedle-dum said Tweedle-dee
    Had spoiled his nice new rattle.
Just then flew by a monstrous crow,
    As big as a tar barrel,
Which frightened both the heroes so,
    They quite forgot their quarrel.

For Every Evil

For every evil under the sun,
There is a remedy, or there is none.
If there be one, try and find it;
If there be none, never mind it.

Little Robin Redbreast

Little Robin Redbreast
   Sat upon a rail;
Niddle naddle went his head,
    Wiggle waggle went his tail.

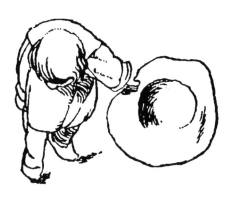

Bumble-Bee

What do I see?
   A bumble-bee
      Sit on a rose
         And wink at me!

      What do you mean
      By hum, hum, hum?
   If you mean me,
I dare not come!

Bat

Bat, bat, come under my hat,
And I'll give you a slice of bacon;
    And when I bake
    I'll give you a cake,
If I am not mistaken.

Pussycat

Pussycat Mole jumped over a coal
    And in her best petticoat burnt a great hole.
Poor pussy's weeping, she'll have no more milk,
    Until her best petticoat's mended with silk.

Little Puppy-Dog

"Come hither, little puppy-dog,
　　I'll give you a new collar,
If you will learn to read a book,
　　And be a clever scholar."
"No! no!" replied the puppy-dog,
　　"I've other fish to fry;
For I must learn to guard your house,
　　And bark when thieves come nigh."

Ba, Ba, Black Sheep

Ba, ba, black sheep,
　　Have you any wool?
Yes, sir, no, sir,
　　Three bags full.
One for my master,
　　And one for my dame,
But none for the little boy
　　Who cries in the lane.

Jack and Jill

Jack and Jill went up the hill
    To fetch a pail of water;
Jack fell down and broke his crown
    And Jill came tumbling after.

Up Jack got and home did trot
    As fast as he could caper,
Dame Jill had the job, to plaster his knob,
    With vinegar and brown paper.

Simple Simon

Simple Simon met a pieman
    Going to the fair;
Says Simple Simon to the pieman,
    "Let me taste your ware."

Says the pieman to Simple Simon,
    "Show me first your penny,"
Says Simple Simon to the pieman,
    "Indeed I have not any."

Simple Simon went a-fishing
    For to catch a whale;
All the water he had got
    Was in his mother's pail.

Little Betty Blue

Little Betty Blue,
Lost her holiday shoe.
    What can little Betty do?
Give her another
To match the other,
    And then she may walk in two.

Little Boy Blue

Little boy blue, come blow your horn,
The sheep's in the meadow, the cow's in the corn;
Where's the little boy that looks after the sheep?
He's under the hay-cock fast asleep.
Will you wake him? No, not I;
For if I do, he'll be sure to cry.

Peter Piper

Peter Piper picked a peck of pickled peppers;
   A peck of pickled peppers Peter Piper picked;
If Peter Piper picked a peck of pickled peppers,
   Where's the peck of pickled peppers Peter
   Piper picked?

Jack-a-Dandy

Handy Spandy, Jack-a-dandy,
Loved plum-cake and sugar-candy;
He bought some at a grocer's shop,
And out he came, hop, hop, hop.

Pease-Pudding

Pease-pudding hot,
    Pease-pudding cold,
Pease-pudding in the pot,
    Nine days old.
Some like it hot,
    Some like it cold,
Some like it in the pot,
    Nine days old.

Hobbledy Hops

Hobbledy Hops,
He made some tops
 Out of the morning-glory;
He used the seed, —
He did indeed,
 And that's the end of my story.

Hi! Diddle Diddle

Hi! diddle diddle,
The cat and the fiddle
   The cow jumped over the moon;
The little dog laughed
To see such sport,
   While the dish ran away with the spoon.

If All the World

If all the world were apple pie,
    And all the sea were ink,
And all the trees were bread and cheese,
    What should we have to drink?

Sing a Song of Sixpence

Sing a song of sixpence,
    A pocket full of rye;
Four and twenty blackbirds
    Baked in a pie.

When the pie was opened
    The birds began to sing;
Was not that a dainty dish
    To set before the king?

The king was in the counting-house
    Counting out his money;
The queen was in the parlour
    Eating bread and honey;

The maid was in the garden
    Hanging out the clothes,
There came a little blackbird
    And snapped off her nose.

Corporal Tim

Corporal Tim
Was dressed so trim,
He thought them all afraid of him;
    But sad to say
    The very first day
    We had a fight
    He died of fright,
And that was the end of Corporal Tim.

Greedy Jane

"Pudding *and* pie,"
Said Jane; "O my!"
"Which would you rather?"
Said her father.
"Both!" cried Jane,
Quite bold and plain.

King Pippin's Hall

King Pippin he built a fine new hall,
Pastry and piecrust that was the wall;
The windows were made of black pudding
    and white,
Slated with pancakes, — you ne'er saw the like.

Fiddle-De-Dee

Fiddle-de-dee, fiddle-de-dee,
The fly has married the bumble-bee;
They went to church, and married was she
The fly has married the bumble-bee.

Thomas a Tattamus

Thomas a Tattamus took two T's,
To tie two tups to two tall trees,
To frighten the terrible Thomas a Tattamus!
Tell me how many T's there are in all THAT!

When I Was a Little Boy

When I was a little boy
    I had but little wit;
It is some time ago
    And I've no more yet.

Foxy's Hole

Put your finger in Foxy's hole,
    Foxy is not at home:
Foxy is at the back door,
    Picking of a bone.

The Man in the Wilderness

The man in the wilderness asked me,
How many strawberries grew in the sea?
I answered him as I thought good,
As many red herrings grew in the wood.

The Lion and the Unicorn

The Lion and the Unicorn
    Were fighting for the crown;
The Lion beat the Unicorn
    All round about the town,
Some gave them white bread,
    And some gave them brown;
Some gave them plum-cake,
    And sent them out of town.

The Man in the Moon

The man in the moon
    Came down too soon,
And asked his way to Norwich:
    He went by the south,
    And burnt his mouth
With eating cold plum-porridge.

The Crooked Man

There was a crooked man, and he went
    A crooked mile.
He found a crooked sixpence against
    A crooked stile:
He bought a crooked cat, which caught
    A crooked mouse,
And they all lived together in
    A little crooked house.

Spell Potatoes
without any Letters

Put 1 0; put 2 0's; put 3 0's;
Put 4 0's; put 5 0's; put 6 0's;
Put 7 0's; put 8 0's, — Potatoes!

The Old Woman

There was an old woman
    Lived under a hill;
And if she's not gone,
    She lives there still.

The Wise Men of Gotham

Three wise men of Gotham
Went to sea in a bowl:
And if the bowl had been stronger,
My song would have been longer.

Cranberry Pies

There was an old woman lived under a hill;
  And if she's not gone, she lives there still.
Baked apples she sold, and cranberry pies,
  And she's the old woman who never told lies.

Molly and I

Molly, my sister, and I fell out,
And what do you think it was about?
She loved coffee, and I loved tea,
And that was the reason we couldn't agree.

I Had a Little Husband

I had a little husband
　　No bigger than my thumb;
I put him in a pint pot,
　　And there I bid him drum.

I bought him a little horse,
　　That galloped up and down.
I bridled him and saddled him,
　　And sent him out of town.

I gave him some garters,
　　To garter up his hose,
And a little handkerchief,
　　To wipe his pretty nose.

A Cottage in Fife

In a cottage in Fife
Lived a man and his wife
    Who, believe me, were comical folk;
For to people's surprise,
They both saw with their eyes,
    And their tongues moved whenever
    they spoke.

Duke O' York

O, the grand old Duke O' York,
    He had ten thousand men;
He marched them up the hill my boys,
    Then marched them down again!
So, when you're up, you're up,
    And when you're down, you're down;
And when you're neither down nor up,
    You're neither up nor down.

There was a Little Girl

There was a little girl who wore a little hood,
    And a curl down the middle of her forehead;
When she was good, she was very, very good,
    But when she was bad, she was horrid.

Elizabeth, Elspeth, Betsy, and Bess

Elizabeth, Elspeth, Betsy, and Bess,
They all went together to seek a bird's nest;
They found a bird's nest with five eggs in,
They all took one and left four in.

A Farmer Went Trotting

A farmer went trotting upon his grey mare,
    Bumpety, bumpety, bump!
With his daughter behind him so rosy and fair,
    Lumpety, lumpety, lump!

A raven cried croak! and they all tumbled down
    Bumpety, bumpety, bump!
The mare broke her knees, and the farmer his
crown,
    Lumpety, lumpety, lump!

The mischievous raven flew laughing away,
    Bumpety, bumpety, bump!
And vowed he would serve them the same the
next day,
    Lumpety, lumpety, lump!

Foot Soldiers

'Tis all the way to Toe-town,
    Beyond the Knee-high hill,
That Baby has to travel down
    To see the soldiers drill.

One, two, three, four five, a-row —
    A captain and his men —
And on the other side, you know,
    Are six, seven, eight, nine, ten.

The Teeth

Thirty white horses upon a red hill,
Now they tramp, now they champ,
   Now they stand still.

Evening

Evening red and morning gray,
It is the sign of a bonnie day;
Evening gray and morning red,
The lamb and the ewe go wet to bed.

March Winds
and April Showers

March winds and April showers
Bring forth May flowers.

Evening red and morning gray
Set the traveller on his way;

But evening gray and morning red,
Bring the rain upon his head.

Rain

The rain is raining all around,
It falls on field and tree,
It rains on the umbrellas here,
And on the ships at sea.

Blow, Wind, Blow!

Blow, wind, blow! and go, mill, go!
    That the miller may grind his corn;
That the baker may take it and into rolls make it,
    And send us some hot in the morn.

Stay at Home

If bees stay at home,
Rain will soon come;
If they fly away,
Fine will be the day.

The Five Little Fairies

Said this little fairy,
"I'm as thirsty as can be!"

Said this little fairy,
"I'm hungry, too! dear me!"

Said this little fairy,
"Who'll tell us where to go?"

Said this little fairy,
"I'm sure that I don't know!"

Said this little fairy,
"Let's brew some Dew-drop Tea!"

So they sipped it and ate honey
Beneath the maple tree.

What Do You Look For?

What do you look for, what do you seek?
  A silver bird with a golden beak.

What do you long for, what do you crave?
  Golden gems in a silver cave.

What do you lack, and what do you need?
  A silver sword and a golden steed.

What do you want, of what do you dream?
  A golden ship on a silver stream.

What do you have, and what do you own?
  A silver robe and a golden crown.

What would you be? Oh, what would you be?
  Only the king of the land and sea.

Where I Would Be!

Oh, that I was where I would be!
Then I would be where I am not!
But where I am, I must be,
And where I would be I cannot.

Matthew, Mark, Luke and John

Matthew, Mark, Luke and John,
Guard the bed that I lie on!
    Four corners to my bed,
    Four angels round my head —
One to watch, one to pray,
And two to bear my soul away.

The Little Star

Twinkle, twinkle, little star,
How I wonder what you are;
Up above the world, so bright,
Like a diamond in the night.

When the blazing sun is gone,
When he nothing shines upon,
Then you show your little light,
Twinkle, twinkle, all the night.

Then the traveller in the dark,
Thanks you for your tiny spark;
He could not tell which way to go
If you did not twinkle so.

In the dark blue sky you keep,
And often through my curtains peep;
For you never shut your eye
Till the sun is in the sky.

As your bright and tiny spark
Lights the traveller in the dark,
Though I know not what you are,
Twinkle, twinkle, little star.

Oh! Look at the Moon

Oh! look at the moon,
    She is shining up there;
Oh! mother, she looks
    Like a lamp in the air.

Last week she was smaller,
    And shaped like a bow;
But now she's grown bigger,
    And round as an O.

Pretty moon, pretty moon,
    How you shine on the door,
And make it all bright
    On my nursery floor!

You shine on my playthings,
    And show me their place,
And I love to look up
    At your pretty bright face.

And there is a star
    Close by you, and may be
That small, twinkling star
    Is your little baby.

Around the World

In go-cart so tiny
    My sister I drew;
And I've promised to draw her
    The wide world through.

We have not yet started —
    I own it with sorrow —
Because our trip's always
    Put off 'till tomorrow.

As I Was Going to St. Ives

As I was going to St. Ives,
I met a man with seven wives;
Every wife had seven sacks,
Every sack had seven cats,
Every cat had seven kits —
Kits, cats, sacks, and wives,
How many were going to St. Ives?

Ride a Cock-Horse

Ride a cock-horse to Banbury Cross,
To see an old lady upon a white horse,
Rings on her fingers, and bells on her toes,
And so she makes music wherever she goes.

Little Bo-Peep

Little Bo-peep has lost her sheep,
    And can't tell where to find them;
Leave them alone, and they'll come home,
    And bring their tails behind them.

Little Bo-peep fell fast asleep,
    And dreamt she heard them bleating;
And when she awoke, she found it a joke,
    For they were still all fleeting.

Then up she took her little crook,
    Determin'd for to find them;
She found them indeed, but it made her heart
bleed,
    For they'd left all their tails behind 'em.

Merry Go the Bells

Merry go the bells, and merry do they ring,
Merry was myself, and merry did I sing;
With a merry ding-dong, ding-a-ling, dee,
And a merry sing-song, merry let us be!

Waddle goes your gait, and hollow are your hose,
Noddle goes you pate, and nodding is your nose;
Merry is your sing-song, ding-a-ling, dee,
With a merry ding-dong, merry let us be!

Merry have we met, and merry have we been,
Merry let us part, and merry meet again;
With a merry sing-song, ding-a-ling, dee,
And a merry ding-dong, merry let us be!

Jacky, Come Give Me the Fiddle

Jacky, come give me the fiddle,
    If ever thou mean to thrive.
Nay, I'll not give my fiddle
    To any man alive.

If I should give my fiddle
    They'll think that I'm gone mad,
For many a joyful day
    My fiddle and I have had.

Lilies are White

Lilies are white,
Rosemary's green;
When you are king,
I will be queen.

Roses are red,
Lavender's blue;
If you will have me,
I will have you.

Monday's Child

Monday's child is fair of face,
Tuesday's child is full of grace,
Wednesday's child is full of woe,
Thursday's child has far to go,
Friday's child is loving and giving,
Saturday's child works hard for its living,
And a child that's born on the Sabbath day
Is fair and wise and good and gay.

Marvels

If all the seas were one sea,
What a great sea that would be!
If all the trees were one tree,
What a great tree that would be!
And if all the axes were one axe,
What a great axe that would be!
And if all the men were one man,
What a great man that would be!
And if the great man took the great axe,
And cut down the great tree
And let it fall into the great sea,
What a splish-splash *that* would be!

Moon, So Round and Yellow

Moon, so round and yellow,
    Looking from on high,
How I love to see you
    Shining in the sky.
Oft and oft I wonder,
    When I see you there,
How they get to light you,
    Hanging in the air:

Where you go at morning,
    When the night is past,
And the sun comes peeping
    O'er the hills at last.
Sometimes I will watch you
    Slyly overhead,
When you think I'm sleeping
    Snugly in my bed.

Of All the Gay Birds

Of all the gay birds that e'er I did see,
The owl is the fairest by far to me;
For all the day long she sits on a tree,
And when the night comes away flies she.
    To-whit, To-whoo,
    Sir knave to you,
Her song is well sung, To-whit, To-whoo.

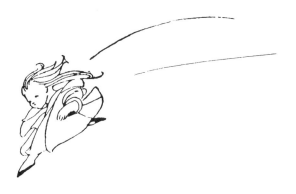

Little Folded Hands

Two little folded hands, soft and brown,
Two little eyelids cast meekly down,
And two little angels guard him in bed,
"One at the foot, and one at the head."

When Mary Goes Walking

When Mary goes walking,
   The autumn winds blow.
The poplars they curtsey,
   The larches bend low,
The oaks and the beeches
   Their gold they fling down,
To make her a carpet,
   To make her a crown.

The Three Little Kittens

Three little kittens lost their mittens;
  And they began to cry,
  "Oh, mother dear,
  We very much fear
That we have lost our mittens."
  "Lost your mittens!
  You naughty kittens!
Then you shall have no pie."

The three little kittens found their mittens;
  And they began to cry,
  "Oh, mother dear,
  See here, see here!
See, we have found our mittens!"
  "Put on your mittens,
  You silly kittens,
And you may have some pie."
  "Purr-r, purr-r, purr-r,
  Oh, let us have some pie.
  Purr-r, purr-r, purr-r."

The three little kittens put on their mittens,
    And soon ate up the pie.
    "Oh, mother dear,
    We greatly fear
That we have soiled our mittens!"
    "Soiled your mittens!
    You naughty kittens!"
Then they began to sigh,
    "Mee-ow, mee-ow, mee-ow."

The three little kittens washed their mittens,
    And hung them out to dry;
    "Oh, mother dear
    Do you not hear
That we have washed our mittens?"
    "Washed your mittens!
    Oh, you're good kittens!
But I smell a rat close by;
    Hush, hush! mee-ow, mee-ow."
    "We smell a rat close by,
    Mee-ow, mee-ow, mee-ow."

Old Mother Hubbard

Old Mother Hubbard
Went to the cupboard
   To get her poor dog a bone:
But when she came there
The cupboard was bare,
   And so the poor dog had none.

She went to the baker's
To buy him some bread,
   But when she came back
The poor dog was dead.

She went to the joiner's
To buy him a coffin,
   When she came back,
The dog was laughing.

She took a clean dish
To get him some tripe,
   But when she came back
He was smoking a pipe.

She went to the fishmonger's
To buy him some fish,
　　And when she came back
He was licking the dish.

She went to the ale-house
To get him some beer,
　　But when she came back
The dog sat in a chair.

She went to the tavern
For white wine and red,
　　But when she came back
The dog stood on his head.

She went to the hatter's
To buy him a hat,
　　And when she came back
He was feeding the cat.

She went to the barber's
To buy him a wig,
　　But when she came back
He was dancing a jig.

She went to the fruiterer's
To buy him some fruit,
　　But when she came back
He was playing the flute.

She went to the tailor's
To buy him a coat,
　　But when she came back
He was riding a goat.

She went to the cobbler's
To buy him some shoes,
　　But when she came back
He was reading the news.

She went to the seamstress
To buy him some linen,
　　But when she came back
The dog was spinning.

She went to the hosier's
To buy him some hose,
　　But when she came back
He was dressed in his clothes.

The dame made a curtsey,
  The dog made a bow,
The dame said, "your servant,"
  The dog said, "bow-wow."

Index of First Lines